A Platypus' World

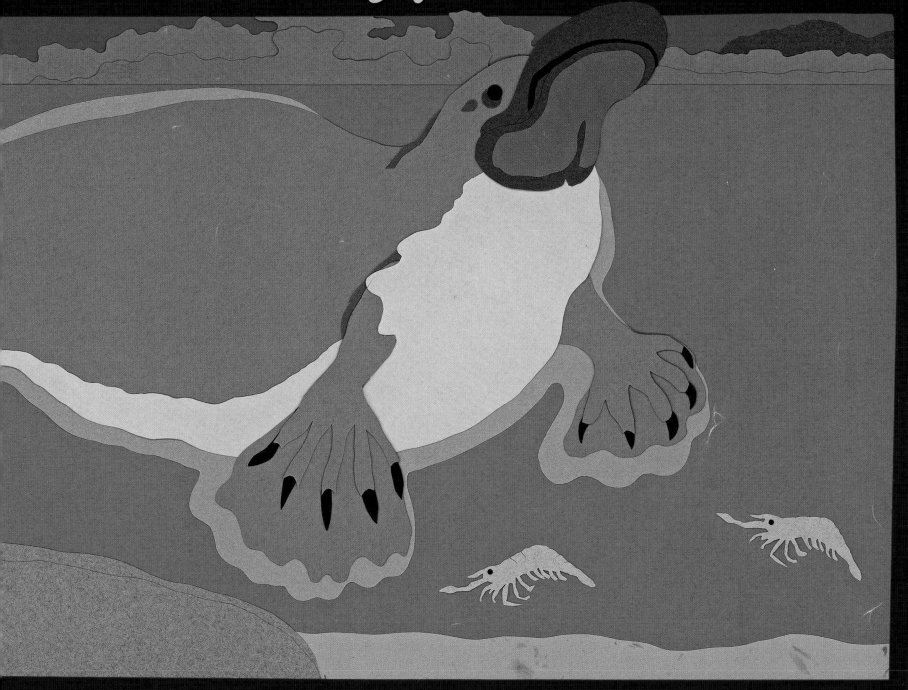

written and illustrated by Caroline Arnold

PICTURE WINDOW BOOKS
Minneapolis, Minnesota

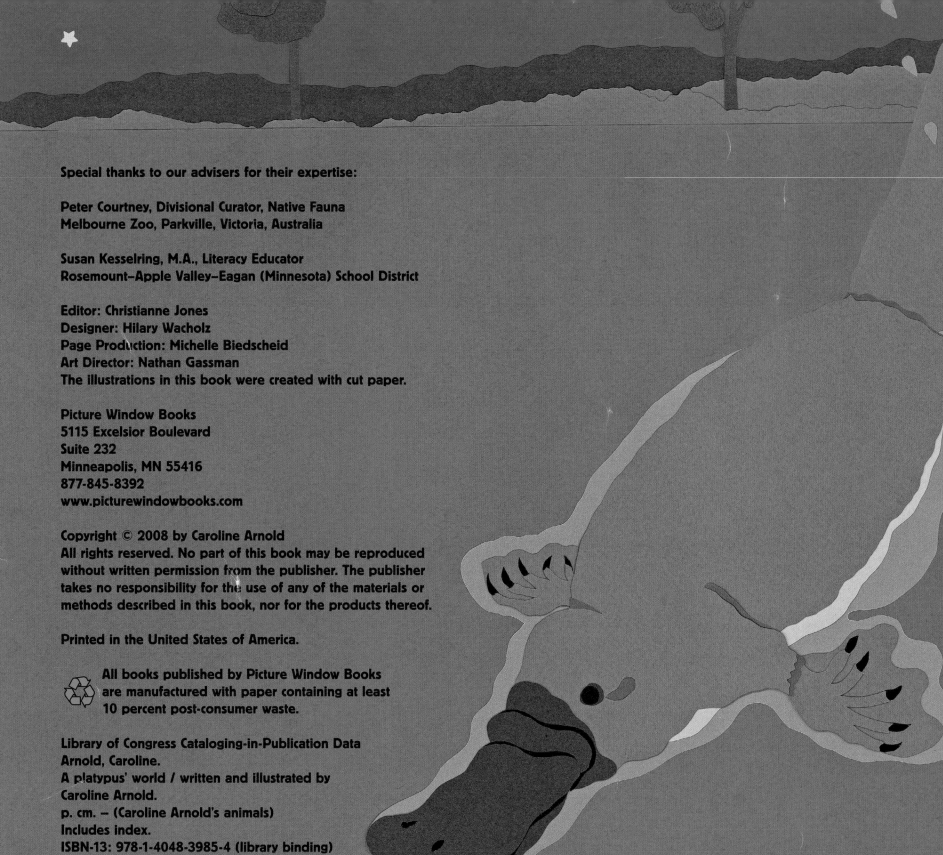

Special thanks to our advisers for their expertise:

Peter Courtney, Divisional Curator, Native Fauna
Melbourne Zoo, Parkville, Victoria, Australia

Susan Kesselring, M.A., Literacy Educator
Rosemount–Apple Valley–Eagan (Minnesota) School District

Editor: Christianne Jones
Designer: Hilary Wacholz
Page Production: Michelle Biedscheid
Art Director: Nathan Gassman
The illustrations in this book were created with cut paper.

Picture Window Books
5115 Excelsior Boulevard
Suite 232
Minneapolis, MN 55416
877-845-8392
www.picturewindowbooks.com

Printed in the United States of America.

All books published by Picture Window Books
are manufactured with paper containing at least
10 percent post-consumer waste.

Library of Congress Cataloging-in-Publication Data
Arnold, Caroline.
A platypus' world / written and illustrated by
Caroline Arnold.
p. cm. – (Caroline Arnold's animals)
Includes index.
ISBN-13: 978-1-4048-3985-4 (library binding)
1. Platypus–Australia–Juvenile literature. I. Title.
QL737.M72A76 2008
599.2'9–dc22   2007032890

The Platypus

Where it lives: Australia

Habitat: edges of streams, rivers, and lakes

Food: worms, insects, fish eggs, water plants, and other small aquatic life

Length: males average 20 inches (51 centimeters); females average 17 inches (43 cm)

Weight: males up to 4.8 pounds (2.2 kilograms); females up to 4.4 pounds (2 kg)

Animal class: mammals

Scientific name: *Ornithorhynchus anatinus*

A platypus is an unusual kind of mammal called a monotreme [MAH-nuh-treem]. Monotremes are mammals that lay eggs. Follow a mother platypus and her two babies and learn about a platypus' world.

It is a warm spring night in an Australian woodland. At the edge of a stream, a platypus comes out of her burrow. Her wide bill and webbed feet make her look a bit like a duck. Her broad tail and thick fur make her look a bit like a beaver. This strange animal is at home on land and in the water.

green and
gold frog

A platypus burrow may be up to 60 feet (18.3 meters) long.
The platypus rests there during the day and comes out at night.

Splash! **The platypus dives into the cool water. She paddles with her front feet and steers with her back feet and tail. All night long, she searches for worms, shrimp, and insects to eat.**

6

As she swims along the bottom of the stream, she sweeps her bill from side to side. When she finds some food, she grabs it in her bill. Then she tucks it into a pouch inside her cheek.

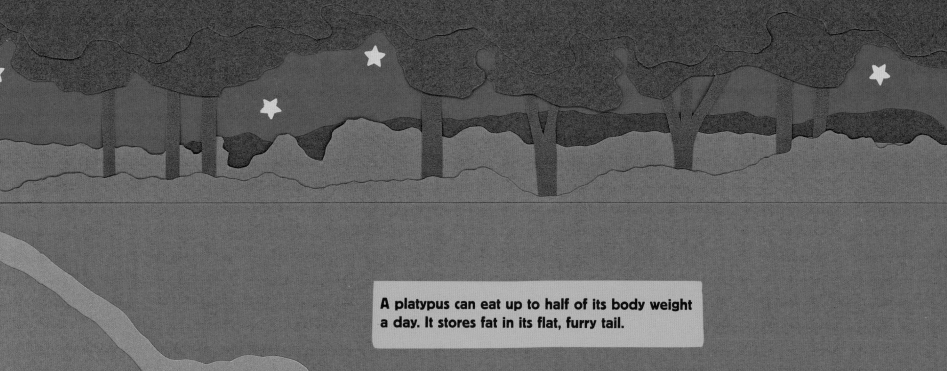

A platypus can eat up to half of its body weight a day. It stores fat in its flat, furry tail.

horsehair worms

caddisfly larvae

freshwater shrimp

The platypus' cheek pouches are full of food. She swims to the top of the water and floats. The platypus has no teeth. Instead, she crushes the food between small pads in her jaws.

Tonight there is another platypus in the stream. He will mate with the female and leave. In less than a month, the female platypus will be ready to lay eggs.

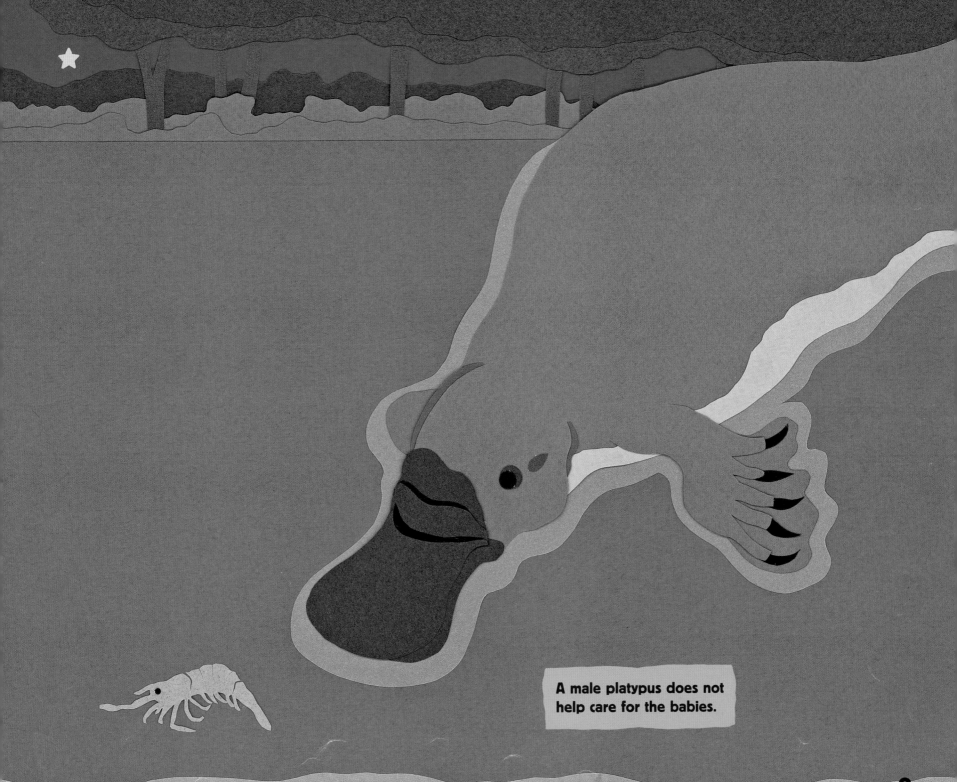

A male platypus does not help care for the babies.

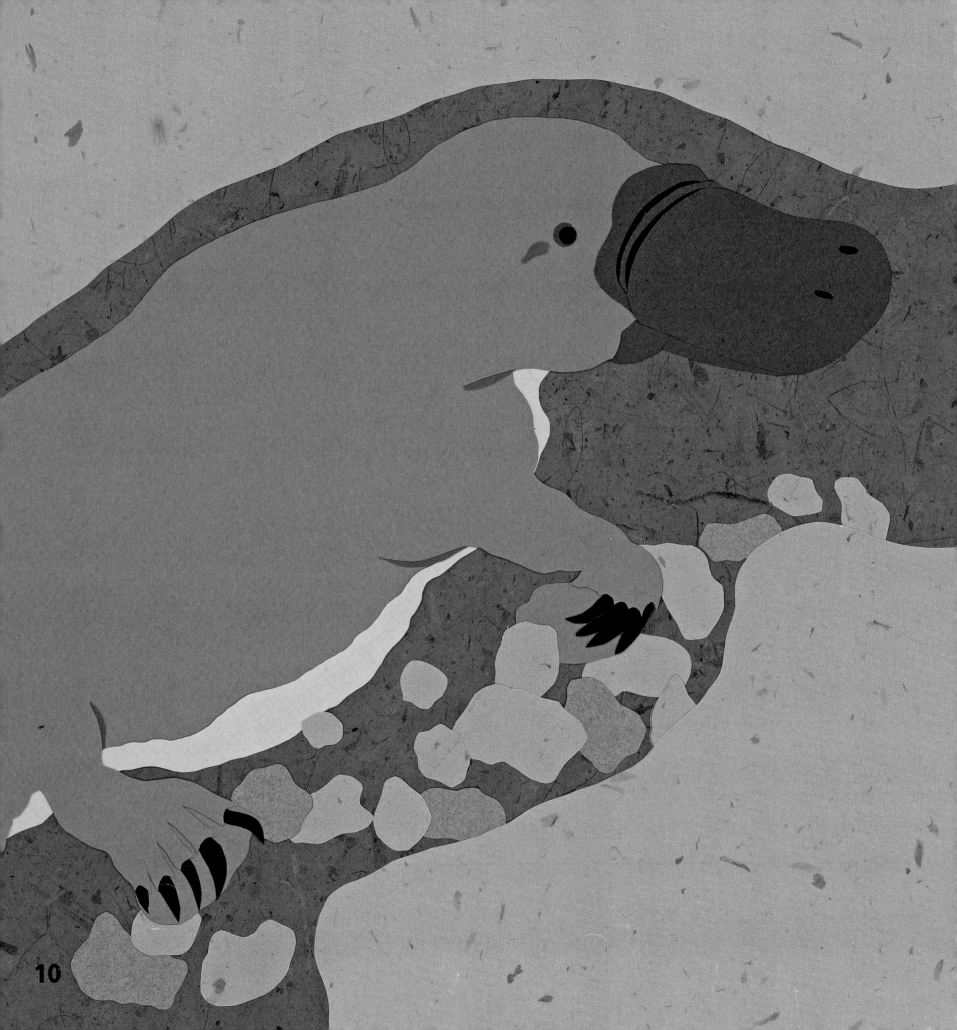

The female platypus digs a new burrow. She folds back the webs on her front feet. Her sharp claws dig into the dirt. Her flat tail pushes the loose dirt out of the way. At the end of the tunnel, she makes a cozy room. She lines it with leaves. This will be her nest.

A platypus may have several burrows. One is for nesting, and the others are for resting.

The platypus blocks the entrance to her nesting burrow with mud and damp leaves. Then she lays two tiny, white eggs. They stick to the fur on her belly.

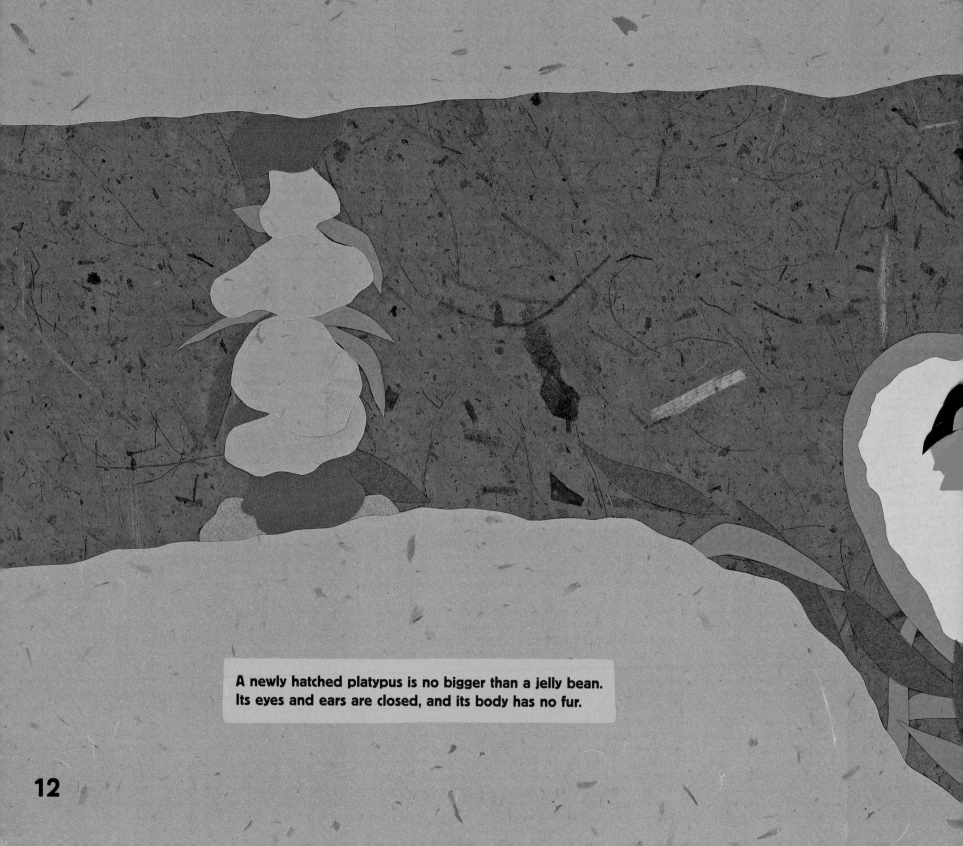

A newly hatched platypus is no bigger than a jelly bean. Its eyes and ears are closed, and its body has no fur.

Ten days later, two baby platypuses push their way out of their eggs. They snuggle up against their mother's belly. They drink milk that comes out of tiny holes in her skin.

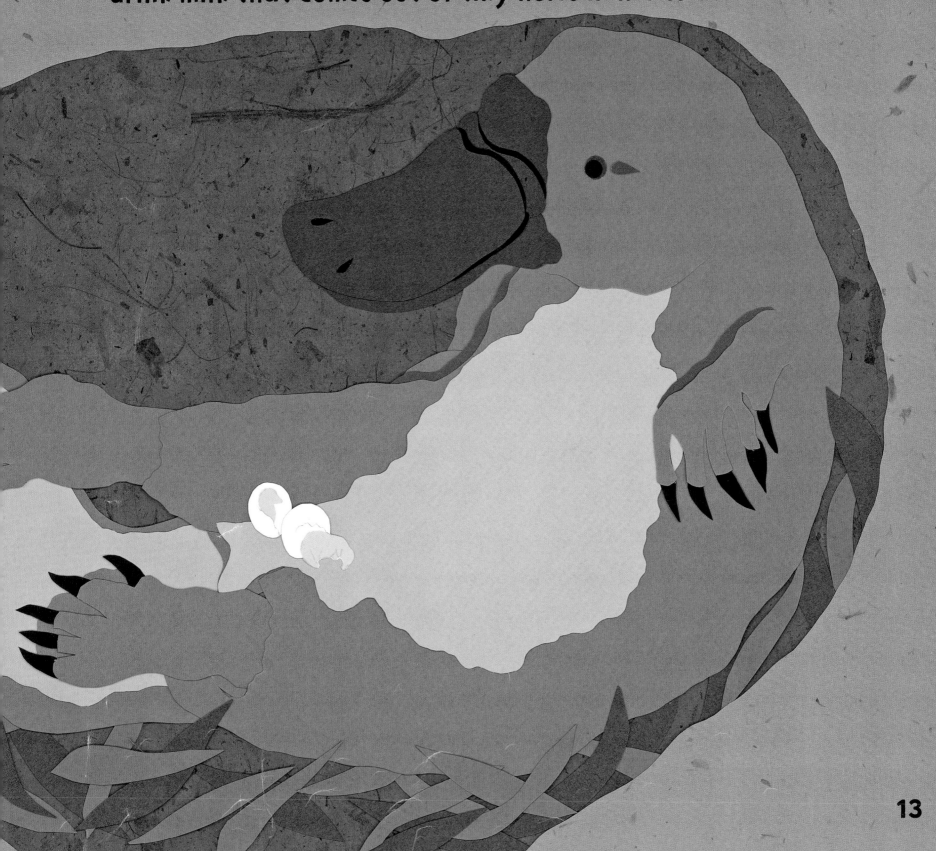

powerful owl

red fox

The mother platypus is hungry, too. She leaves her babies in the nest and goes to hunt for food.

When she is out of the burrow, she must watch out for danger. *Whoo! Whoo!* An owl is nearby. The platypus hurries back to the safety of the burrow.

Foxes, dingoes, and owls are the main predators of the platypus.

The baby platypuses grow quickly. By 6 weeks, they have fur, and their eyes are open. At 14 weeks, they are ready to explore. They follow their mother to the edge of the stream. While she hunts for food, they grunt and squeak as they play along the shore.

A 6-week-old platypus is about 12 inches (30 cm) long.

Soon the young platypuses are ready for their first swim. *Splish! Splash!* They dive into the water. Thick fur keeps their skin warm and dry.

At first, their mother catches food and shares it with them. As the young platypuses get older, they learn to find their own food.

A platypus breathes air like other mammals. Its nostrils are at the front of its bill.

Now the young platypuses are 5 months old. They are nearly as big as their mother. They no longer drink milk and can find their own food. They are ready to be on their own. They will dig their own burrows.

In another year and a half, they will be ready to mate and have their own babies. Then the splash of new platypuses will be heard in the night.

Where do platypuses live?

Platypuses are widespread in the eastern parts of mainland Australia. In Tasmania, the platypus is common in the lakes of the Central Highlands. It is also seen in rivers and streams of the south, southwest, and northwest coasts.

INDIAN OCEAN

PACIFIC OCEAN

NORTHERN TERRITORY

AUSTRALIA

QUEENSLAND

WESTERN AUSTRALIA

SOUTH AUSTRALIA

NEW SOUTH WALES

VICTORIA

SOUTHERN OCEAN

TASMANIA

THE YELLOW PART OF THE MAP SHOWS WHERE PLATYPUSES LIVE

Platypus Fun Facts

Good Divers

A platypus may dive up to 80 times an hour. When feeding, it stays underwater for 20 to 40 seconds at a time. When resting, it can stay underwater for up to 14 minutes.

Soft Bills

The platypus' wide bill is made of cartilage, the same material you have in your nose. It is soft and can bend. The bill is covered with skin.

Poison Spurs

The male platypus has a sharp spur, or claw, on each hind leg. It is filled with poison. He uses the spurs for defense against natural enemies and for fighting other males.

Long Lives

Platypuses can live at least 10 years in the wild and 20 years in zoos.

An Electric Sense

A platypus closes its eyes while diving. It finds food by feeling small amounts of electricity produced by the animals it feeds on.

Double-Thick Fur

A platypus has two layers of fur, a thick, woolly undercoat and long fur on top. The fur traps air next to the skin, so the animal's body stays dry, even while diving.

Glossary

aquatic—*growing or living in water all or most of the time*

cartilage—*the strong, bendable material in the body*

dingoes—*wild dogs that live in Australia*

habitat—*the place or natural conditions in which a plant or animal lives*

mammals—*warm-blooded animals that feed their babies milk*

mate—*to join together to produce young*

monotremes—*mammals that lay eggs; the platypus and echidna, or spiny anteater, are the world's only monotremes*

nostrils—*holes in the nose that let air go in and out*

predators—*animals that hunt and eat other animals*

spur—*a pointed object used to prod or poke*

To Learn More

More Books to Read

Clarke, Ginjer. *Platypus!* New York: Random House Books for Young Readers, 2004.

Collard, Sneed. *A Platypus, Probably.* Watertown, Mass.: Charlesbridge Publishing, 2005.

Short, Joan. *Platypus.* New York: Mondo Publishing, 1997.

On the Web

FactHound offers a safe, fun way to find Web sites related to topics in this book. All of the sites on FactHound have been researched by our staff.

1. Visit *www.facthound.com*

2. Type in this special code: 1404839852

3. Click on the FETCH IT button.

Your trusty FactHound will fetch the best sites for you!

Index

bill, 4, 7, 19, 23
burrow, 4, 5, 11, 12, 14, 20
cheek pouch, 7, 8
claws, 11, 23
dig, 11, 20
diving, 6, 18, 23
eggs, 3, 9, 12, 13
eyes, 12, 16
feet, 4, 6, 11
fur, 4, 12, 16, 18, 23
mammal, 3, 19
mating, 9, 21
milk, 13, 20
monotreme, 3
nest, 11, 12, 14
predators, 15
swimming, 7, 8, 18
tail, 4, 6, 7, 11
woodland, 4

Look for all of the books in Caroline Arnold's Animals series:

A Kangaroo's World
A Killer Whale's World
A Koala's World
A Panda's World
A Penguin's World
A Platypus' World
A Wombat's World
A Zebra's World